Original title:
Green Veins

Copyright © 2025 Creative Arts Management OÜ
All rights reserved.

Author: Amelia Montgomery
ISBN HARDBACK: 978-1-80567-040-7
ISBN PAPERBACK: 978-1-80567-120-6

The Swaying Embrace

In the garden, plants do dance,
With their leaves, they take a chance.
Swinging to the rhythm of the breeze,
Bunny hops and zigzag tease.

Worms throw a party underground,
Laughing as they twist and wind.
Sunflowers waving high above,
Just don't bring the hungry dove!

Flourishing Lines

I doodled on the soil so deep,
With muddy fingers, oh so cheap.
The daisies giggled, laughing loud,
As I painted shapes like a clownish crowd.

Cactus tried to join the fun,
But pricked himself on a sunny run.
Petunias threw petals in the air,
Their colorful confetti, beyond compare!

Pulse of the Biome

Bees buzz around like tiny cars,
Trying to catch the rhythm of stars.
A frog croaks tunes by the pond,
While crickets chirp, and respond.

The trees gossip in whispers so sly,
Under their limbs, owls blink and fly.
Nature's got a show tonight,
With laughter echoing under moonlight!

Organic Whisperings

Listen close to the garden's glee,
As veggies giggle in jubilee.
Carrots tell tales beneath the mud,
While radishes shake in a cheerful flood.

The lettuce quips, so crisp and wise,
While cucumbers roll with secret sighs.
A squash does stand-up, lovably goofy,
Bringing joy to all, oh so spoofy!

The Roots of Renewal

In the garden, plants laugh loud,
With roots that wiggle, feeling proud.
Worms tell jokes, and leaves all cheer,
Their puns grow greater each passing year.

Bugs wear tiny glasses, oh what a sight,
Sipping nectar, buzzing all night.
Potatoes play hide, seek underground,
While carrots giggle, all safe and sound.

Echoing Ecosystems

The trees gossip in breezy tones,
While frogs croak rhythms on pond-like phones.
Birds start singing their silly tunes,
As flowers dance under bright, silly moons.

Fungi wear hats, mushrooms in style,
They plan tea parties, stay for a while.
The sun beams down with a wink of light,
Making shadows play tag in sheer delight.

Serpentine Stories

A snake that wears glasses slithers with grace,
Telling tall tales of his cozy, warm place.
He claims he met mice who wore tiny shoes,
And danced, while he marveled at their fancy moves.

Lizards jump in, they want to compete,
With cartwheels and flips that can't be beat.
They laugh at the antics of their great friend,
Who swears he could fly, if he'd only pretend.

Vibrant Lifelines

Cacti in hats sit bright in the sun,
Trading their puns, oh, so much fun!
A sunflower stretches and whispers, hey,
"Let's bring the blooms out to play today!"

A ladybug joins, with flair and spin,
As petals form circles, they all jump in.
Life's a grand party in color and cheer,
With laughter and joy throughout the whole year.

Bursting Vitality

In the garden, things do jig,
A cabbage doing a little jig.
Radishes wear tiny hats,
While carrots dance with sassy cats.

Lettuce giggles, blushing bright,
Under the sun, such a delight.
Tomatoes bounce and sing a tune,
While beans play catch with a lazy moon.

Crescendo of Chlorophyll

Broccoli sounds off a pirate's shout,
"Arr matey, these greens are what it's about!"
Spinach flexes its leafy arm,
While kale struts in, bringin' the charm.

Peas roll up in tiny cars,
Commuting through gardens, oh how bizarre!
A mango joins with a flashy spin,
It's a fruit fiesta, let the fun begin!

Climbing Ambrosia

Vines are climbing, seeking fame,
Each leaf whispering a cheeky name.
Zucchini seeks the highest stage,
While squash gets lost in its own page.

Pumpkins throw a party, oh what fun!
"Who brought the seeds?" they shout and run.
With each twist and a topsy turn,
A salad's made, for us to learn!

Elysian Currents

In the realm of leafy delight,
Herbs gossip softly, day and night.
Basil teases with a pungent grin,
Thyme chimes in with a cheeky spin.

The parsley plays its wily tricks,
While chives use puns like magic sticks.
Together they dance, a green parade,
In this garden, joy won't fade!

Verdant Arteries

In the garden, plants do jig,
Roots like ribbons, dance so big.
Worms in bow ties spin about,
'Excuse me!' they squeak, as they shout.

Sunflowers wear their hats so high,
They wave to clouds as they float by.
With every sway, they laugh and prance,
Inviting bees to join the dance.

Tapestry of Growth

Lettuce leaf and carrot stick,
In this patch, they play a trick.
'Hey, Tomato! Catch me quick!'
Said the radish, oh so slick.

Vines are tangled, what a mess,
Pruning shears? We'll never guess.
Pumpkins roll and giggle loud,
The garden's just a giggling crowd.

The Pulse of the Forest

Under leaves, the critters play,
Squirrels leap, they've found a way.
With acorns bouncing like a ball,
They dodge the trees, they never stall.

Mushrooms wear their polka dots,
Tiny hats in nature's plots.
Foxes giggle, "What a scene!"
In the woods, where fun's routine.

Nurtured Connections

Bamboo stands like slender gents,
Throwing shade, with funny rents.
They whisper tales of windy days,
While crickets chuckle in the haze.

One vine tangled with another,
'Let's hold tight! We're like a brother!'
Together they support the trees,
While mockingbirds sing with the breeze.

Flourish Beneath the Arching Canopy

Under leaves that sway and dance,
Squirrels prance in their little pants.
Beneath the boughs, the rabbits roam,
Worried about where to make their home.

The branches laugh, they bend and shake,
As chipmunks in their jackets break.
A party of roots below the ground,
Where the wildest fungi can be found.

Life's Lush Interludes.

In the thicket, a parrot's joke,
Adds laughter where the trees bespoke.
The bushes giggle as the breezes tease,
While daisies dance and tickle knees.

The sunlight slips, a playful sprite,
As insects twirl in sheer delight.
It's quite the bash, beneath the shade,
In nature's club, where fun is made.

Emerald Threads

Woven vines with tales to tell,
They weave the stories quite so well.
A sloth, a hug, and a wide-eyed stare,
Beware the pranks that float in air!

The flowers wear their brightest gowns,
While critters sport their leafy crowns.
Each nook and cranny hums a score,
Of laughter echoing evermore.

Nature's Lattice

The twigs are tangled in grand design,
While butterflies sip on dew so fine.
A raccoon juggles acorns with flair,
As nature's jesters perform with care.

The breeze whispers jokes to the flowers,
Tickling leaves in playful showers.
The fun unfolds under the sun,
In this wild world, we've just begun!

Life's Hidden Pathways

In gardens where the lettuce grows,
The critters dance on tiny toes.
With every step, they seek a snack,
A lettuce leaf, a quick attack.

They plot and scheme from dawn till dusk,
While sipping juice from rusty cask.
The hedgehog whispers, 'Can you see?'
This veggie world is wild and free!

Of hidden paths through leafy maze,
Where every corner prompts a gaze.
They make a race of berry hunts,
While dodging bees in silly stunts.

So join the fun and take your whip,
It's time to laugh, take a wild trip.
For in this realm of leafy cheer,
The heartfelt giggles are quite near.

The Weft of Wilderness

A squirrel scurries, nuts in tow,
He stops to chat with dandelions, though.
'They call me bold, they call me spry,
But I just love to eat and fly!'

The flowers blush, they twist and sway,
In whispers soft, they plan their play.
'Two petals here, a leaf or two,'
'A crown of greens, a joke for you!'

Through tangled stems, the laughter spreads,
As bunnies boast of leafy beds.
With every turn of vines and leaves,
The wilderness bursts, and joy believes.

So take a peek, come join our spree,
Where nature's giggles grow like trees.
In this wild web of funny sights,
You'll find the heart of nature's lights.

Vivid Tangles

In jungles thick with vines galore,
The monkeys swing and loudly roar.
They tumble down, and what do you see?
A parrot laughing, 'Join me, wee!'

Each twist and knot brings giggles forth,
As plants debate their fancied worth.
'Hold on, I'm stuck!' a rat exclaims,
'Adventures here are wild, not tame!'

With colors bright, the world's a jest,
Where every sprout just loves to fest.
The daisies giggle, 'Watch us dance!'
While playful leaves, they whirl and prance.

So plunge right in, don't be afraid,
In vivid tangles, life's parades.
Where every bloom has tales to share,
And laughter echoes in the air.

Serenade of the Sprouts

At dawn, the sprouts begin to sing,
They boast of colors, green's the thing.
A cabbage proclaims, 'I'm dressed so fine!'
While carrots hum, 'Oh, do not whine!'

With little hats of moss and dew,
They take a twirl, a funny view.
'Look at us twinkle, what a sight!'
'Our leafy costumes, snug and tight!'

The garden's choir, a rollicking tune,
Brings laughter bright, like a sunny noon.
Where zucchini jests and beans do dance,
In a leafy ball, they take their chance.

So waltz along this verdant patch,
Join in the fun, don't miss the catch.
The sprouts in harmony sing aloud,
In nature's mirth, we're all so proud!

Lush Pathways

Amidst the leaves, I see a race,
The ants parade, a silly chase.
With tiny hats and marching feet,
They march along, their tune's a treat.

The trees gossip, swaying high,
Whispering secrets as I pass by.
A squirrel cracks jokes, quite absurd,
While birds chirp laughter, a funny word.

The bushes tease, they shift and sway,
Photobombing the sun all day.
Flowers wearing hats, oh so bright,
Dancing silly, what a sight!

In this green world, I stroll and grin,
Nature's humor makes me spin.
So on this path, I'll skip and prance,
With every glance, I join the dance.

The Language of Flora

In the garden, plants gather round,
Mimicking voices, a funny sound.
The daisies giggle, while roses wink,
It's a botanic party, what do you think?

Cacti wear glasses, quite the spiff,
Though poky and prickly, they're a bit of a riff.
Sunflowers chat in sunny tones,
Trading jokes with the old garden gnomes.

Vines entwine like an awkward pair,
Trying hard not to tangle in air.
They trip and tumble, what a scene!
Their leafy antics are truly keen.

Oh, the banter among buds and leaves,
Their silly language, one surely believes.
In every bloom and each wild sprout,
Is laughter waiting, there's never a doubt.

Sinews of the Wild

The forest stretches, muscles flex,
Roots like biceps, what a perplex!
With trunks that flex and branches sway,
Even in nature, there's a gym play!

Bamboo's limber, like an acrobat,
It bends and bows, imagine that!
Moss is the mat for a yoga class,
While ferns do downward dog with sass.

The willows laugh, they waddle and sway,
Throwing a shade that's here to stay.
While the tough oak tells jokes so dry,
Pretending it's serious, oh my, oh my!

So in this wild with sinewed grace,
Nature's humor finds its place.
With every leaf a chuckle stirs,
In this green gym, we're all the hers!

Essence of Eden

In Eden's heart, where laughter blooms,
Fruits tell tales with giggly zooms.
The apples blush, their secrets shared,
While bananas swing, unprepared!

Carrots chat from underground,
Making puns without a sound.
The radishes shrug, sparkling with cheer,
As pumpkins joke, 'We're all here!'

The herbs smell sweet, a playful scent,
Dill mischief, with such intent.
Thyme is the joker, oh so sly,
With every leaf, a wink, oh my!

So here in Eden, joy's the theme,
Every plant recounts a funny dream.
With laughter woven through the vines,
This essence of life, forever shines.

Lush Currents and Shadows

In the forest, squirrels dance,
They plot their nutty romance,
While leaves tickle the breeze,
Swaying like they'll never cease.

A wise old tree cracks a joke,
"Why did the branch want to poke?
Because it's tired of standing still,
And craves a laugh, oh what a thrill!"

Mossy carpets tickle toes,
As critters strike up grandiose shows,
With every rustle, giggles rise,
In this green world full of surprise.

Frogs wear hats, they sing with glee,
While vines swing wildly from a tree,
Nature's circus is a blast,
Where every moment's fun amassed.

Symphony of Hidden Roots

Roots play instruments underground,
Tickling worms, what a vibrant sound!
Each ingrained twist sings a tune,
Beneath the shine of a giggling moon.

A beetle conductor leads the show,
While mushrooms giggle, head to toe,
"Do we really make the perfect stew?"
In this wild orchestra, who knew?

The daffodils sway their heads,
Telling tales of garden spreads,
"Have you heard? Peeled potatoes sing,
But only on a sunny spring!"

As laughter bubbles through the loam,
Even snails decide to roam,
In a symphony both silly and serene,
Together swaying in the unseen.

Journey Through Verdant Archways

Through leafy doors we wander wide,
Where giggles echo, and frogs confide,
"Do you think the trees ever sneeze?
Or are they so wise, they stay at ease?"

A rabbit hops in patterned leaps,
Waving to the world, no peeps,
"Catch me if you can, I dare!"
With mischief brewing in the air.

Pinecone hats upon their heads,
All the woodland critters said,
"Let's throw a party, complete with cake,
For the shyest turtle, make no mistake!"

Adventurous paths twist and turn,
While dandelions laugh and churn,
In this riotous theatre of greens,
Where nature pranks and frolics reign supreme.

The Breath Beneath the Foliage

The wind whispers secrets bold,
To the laughing leaves, stories told,
"Did you hear the gossip from the ground?
Earthworms are kings—they wear crowns!"

Butterflies wear polka dot vests,
As they flutter and host a jest,
"Why did the flower take a nap?
To dream of splendor—a flowery wrap!"

Underneath the leafy treasure,
Lies a world bursting with pleasure,
"Let's throw a bash, with roots as friends,
And dance until the sunlight ends!"

So join this wild, whimsical spree,
Where every flap and wiggle's free,
In the breath of nature's playful ways,
Resides a joy that never decays.

Secrets Woven in Botanical Layers

In the garden, tongues do wag,
Plants gossip as I pull a rag.
Whispers float on fragrant air,
'Watch your toes!' they giggle, fair.

Roots entangled, secrets kept,
While I fumble, nearly wept.
'Is that a weed or just my luck?'
The daisies snicker, 'Oh, what's up?'

Sunlight dances on the leaves,
Every rustle, laughter weaves.
'That bug's a dancer, look at him!'
The tulips burst in petals, prim!

I swear these plants have seen it all,
From my trip last spring to fall.
If they could talk, oh what a show!
But they just nod, in greenish glow.

Tidal Flow of Earth's Sprite

Leaves surf the breeze with sheer delight,
Trying to catch a glimpse of flight.
Whimsical sprites jump on the scene,
Chasing shadows, oh so keen!

The garden's tide, it swells and sways,
As I dodge the muddy sprays.
'Checkpoint: find the errant snail!'
They croak and laugh, 'Now that's a tale!'

Roots roll like waves in a silent smirk,
Poking fun, they never shirk.
'Need a hand, or maybe roots?'
The daisies grin in their funny suits.

Earth's laughter echoes all around,
With each rustle, a joyful sound.
Giggles bubble from puddles clear,
Nature's jesters, never fear!

The Hidden Pulse of Wilderness

In shadows thick, mischief hides,
A squirrel steals while the bird abides.
The bark chuckles, sturdy and wise,
'Check this out! No one spies!'

Jumpy frogs on lily pads leap,
While me, tripping, make a heap.
'Hoo, the oak just laughed so loud!'
'Of course, he's wise!' the pebbles bowed.

The trail twitters with tales to tell,
Of clumsy hikers, oh so well.
'Watch your head! That branch is mean!'
'And you thought it was a routine!'

A pulse beats in this leafy maze,
Laughter echoes, lights ablaze.
So when you hike, just be so clear,
The wilderness will bring good cheer!

Veils of Vitality Amongst the Green

In a cloak of hues so bright,
Nature plays, a comical sight.
With petals sprinkled like confetti,
Bumblebees whirl, all unsteady!

The bushes wave, a merry band,
While I trip over what they planned.
'Forget the flowers!' the daisies shout,
'You're the best joke, don't pout!'

Little critters, oh what a crew,
Creating chaos, just for a view.
'Look at that guy, no idea at all!'
They roll and tumble, have a ball.

From sprigs of thyme to mighty oak,
The laughter rises, a swirling smoke.
Vitality veils the everyday scene,
While I laugh loud, 'Ain't this green?'

Boundless Canopies

In a world of leafy thrills,
Where trees tell jokes and do their frills,
Squirrels giggle in the breeze,
While ants dance on the bark with ease.

A monkey swings from branch to branch,
Wearing sunglasses, what a chance!
He slips and lands in a patch of moss,
And all the forest laughs, what a toss!

The sun peeks through with a cheeky grin,
While flowers whisper, 'Let's begin!'
Hedgehogs play a game of tag,
And ladybugs join with a wag.

Oh, the canopy above is filled with cheer,
Where every rustle brings a dear,
So climb aboard this leafy ride,
And revel in the forest's pride.

Ancestral Lifeblood

With roots that tickle the ground below,
Old trees gossip, putting on a show,
'Oh, did you hear? The oak's a dad!'
The pines chime in, 'How can that be sad?'

Every twig's a family tale so grand,
Of sap and sunshine, a hearty band,
While fungi hold their annual ball,
Where even the weeds get a curtain call.

So come dance with the grasses so spry,
As daisies spin and give it a try,
With roots entwined in a quirky jest,
Nature's family reunion is the best!

Where branches sway and laughter blends,
Every creature on the leaf descends,
With the ants as the choir singing rhymes,
This ancestral lifeblood knits good times.

The Essence of Enchantment

In a garden where the colors collide,
Where petals giggle and bees take pride,
A butterfly's wearing a bright tutu,
Saying, 'Look at me, I'm fancy too!'

The soil is rich, full of quirky charms,
It whispers secrets, it hugs with arms,
While gnomes play cards and fairies cheer,
As the moon decides to join them near.

Dew drops are jewels on every leaf,
While rabbits hop with a sense of grief,
'Did you see that carrot? It ran away!'
All creatures chuckle at the game they play.

So dance along this enchanted space,
Where laughter blooms and wins the race,
Roots and blooms, entwined in a song,
In the essence of enchantment, we all belong.

Rich Tapestry

A quilt of green with patches of fun,
Where stories of nature are whimsically spun,
Grasshoppers barding their tales of flight,
While snails slide in, keeping it light.

In this rich tapestry, colors collide,
As worms hold a meeting, all sit side by side,
Should we wear hats or fancy attire?
The spider winks, 'Let's set them on fire!'

Flowers trade petals; who wore it best?
The daisies giggle, 'It's all in jest!'
Mice throw a party, it's quite the bash,
With cheese balloons that go in a flash.

Rippling laughter weaves through the green,
This tapestry's lively, vibrant, and keen,
From roots to petals, each has a role,
In nature's quilt, there's joy in the whole.

Emerald Threads of Life

In a garden where weeds take a dance,
We find a snail in a comical trance.
He glides with flair on a leaf so grand,
Claiming the road, it's his own wonderland.

A worm in a hat thinks he's quite the guy,
Telling tall tales as the ants go by.
"I wriggle and squirm, but I also can charm!"
While grasshoppers chuckle, all safe from harm.

The flowers gossip about bees in a rush,
"Why do they buzz? Are they in a hush?"
With petals aflutter and colors so bright,
They sip on sweet nectar, a thrilling flight.

In this patch of humor, life's quirks we adore,
Where nature's oddities leave us wanting more.
As laughter sprouts with each tender sprig,
Our hearts beat in sync with this leafy jig.

Whispering Canopy Secrets

Beneath the boughs where squirrels debate,
They argue about who's the fastest mate.
With tails like flags and acorn goals,
They race through branches, two nature-controlled souls.

A dove overhears, holds back a caw,
"Is that your new style, or a slip of the paw?"
As nutty disputes go on day after day,
It's hard to keep up with their feathery play.

The breeze joins in with a tickling tease,
It rustles the leaves; even branches feel pleased.
"Hey, can you hear me? I've stories to spin!
From seeds to tall trunks, let the laughter begin!"

So up in the canopy, secrets unfold,
With whispers and giggles that never grow old.
Life's a jest in the branches where they all convene,
An endless comedy, nature's very own scene.

Verdant Pulse of the Earth

In the dirt where the roots play a game,
Plants poke their heads, each calling a name.
They argue like kids on who's the most fun,
"I can grow taller! Just give me some sun!"

Earthworms are digging, with no care to stall,
"We'll show them who rules! We'll work through it all!"
As daisies and dandelions strut with pride,
While toadstools chuckle, with fungus aside.

Rabbits hop past in a jolly parade,
Swapping their stories, in grass they invade.
"Last week I found a great carrot delight,
But I tripped on a twig, oh what a sight!"

In this lively patch, there's much to explore,
With laughter and play, it's never a bore.
From buzzing to blooming, all quirky and spry,
The pulse of the earth makes us chuckle and sigh.

Nature's Lush Embrace

In a field where the daisies decide to unite,
They plan a party for the butterflies' flight.
With petals like banners and sunshine for sound,
They whirl and they twirl, joyfully spellbound.

A hedgehog arrives with a top hat and cheer,
"I'm here to perform! So gather near!"
He sings of adventures that tickle the air,
While the daisies nod, with a blush they all share.

The stream joins the fun, with a gurgling laugh,
"Who wants a drink? I'm nature's photograph!"
With splashes of joy, the frogs leap in mirth,
Each jump is a giggle, pure fun on this earth.

Nature's embrace is a laughter-filled sight,
With colors and sounds that feel just so right.
From whispers of winds to the chirps that we hear,
Every moment in green brings us joy and good cheer.

Wild Whispers

In the garden where the beetles dance,
Frogs in tuxedos take their chance.
Ladybugs laugh, they spin and twirl,
While ants hold meetings, in a loony whirl.

Dandelions puff like fluffy clouds,
While worms sing songs that draw big crowds.
The sunbeams giggle, flicker and glow,
Creating shadow puppets, putting on a show.

Bumblebees buzzing, with a funny hum,
Chasing the flowers, oh what a scrum!
Petunias chuckle in the gentle breeze,
As squirrels play tag, climbing up trees.

The earthworms wiggle in their own parade,
Tickling the roots where sweet fruits are made.
In this jolly patch, mischief is rife,
Nature's own circus, full of life!

Touched by Nature

A leaf in the breeze did a little jig,
While squirrels high-fived, with a nut so big.
The grass was tickled under tiny toes,
As flowers sported hats with frilly bows.

Mushrooms in parties, wearing polka dots,
Swaying like dancers in colorful spots.
The sun winked down, kissing all with glee,
Creating a spectacle for all to see.

Gnomes in the garden, with sly little grins,
Playing hide and seek, as laughter begins.
Each rustle and rumble, a story unspun,
Nature concocts mischief, just for fun.

As daisies gossip, petals flop and sway,
And bees sip nectar in their own ballet.
Every breeze carries giggles and cheer,
In this whimsical realm, nothing to fear!

Seasons of Verdure

In springtime blooms, the laughter ignites,
With bunnies that hop in outrageous tights.
Tulips peek out, in a jovial line,
While robins compete for the best punchline.

Summer brings sun, with mischief in tow,
Ice cream cones melting, what a funny show!
Picnics abound with ants as the guests,
Stealing crumbs, they're the ultimate pests.

Autumn's a riot, colors collide,
Where leaves have fun, on a windy ride.
Pumpkins are giggling, faces so sly,
As scarecrows dance, watching crows fly by.

With winters come snowflakes, a fluffy white flight,
Snowmen with hats, looking quite bright.
Nature's a comedian, always on cue,
With seasons that giggle, just for you!

Interlaced Harmony

In the forest, where the giggles play,
Trees shake hands in a friendly way.
Squirrels do backflips, oh what a sight,
While chipmunks debate who's the cutest by night.

The brook is bubbling with playful glee,
Singing to pebbles, 'Come dance with me!'
Flowers wear crowns of dew-laden charms,
While petals take naps in their leafy arms.

Frogs in tuxedos, croaking a tune,
Under the silver sparkle of the moon.
The stars above chuckle, a wink and a flash,
As crickets create an upbeat bash.

This merry world, where laughter entwines,
Nature's own stories, in whimsical lines.
So join the fun, let your spirits rise,
For in this mad garden, joy never dies!

The Lush Embrace

In the jungle, a leaf had a dream,
To be a salad, a crunchy supreme.
But a squirrel stole it, made a hat,
And now it's a tree's fashionable chat.

A garden party where twigs wear ties,
Dancing with daisies, oh how time flies!
Each branch is a dancer, swaying so free,
With laughter echoing from every tree.

Spirals of Sustenance

There's a carrot that thinks it's a rock star,
Belting out tunes from a cabbage jar.
While radishes giggle and potatoes roll,
Together they form a dig-in patrol!

In this veggie band, I can't help but grin,
Beets on the drums, let the fun begin!
Squash joins in, singing so loud,
Making all of the produce so proud.

Winding Tendrils

A vine decided to twist and twirl,
Chasing butterflies in a glittery whirl.
It tangled a friend, a poor little bee,
Who buzzed and complained, 'Set me free!'

But the vine just laughed, 'Come dance with me!'
'We'll turn this garden into a jubilee!'
They wobbled and jiggled, pure silly delight,
As flowers all giggled at their prancing sight.

Vines of Vitality

Upon a trellis, a grape hangs tight,
Wishing to swing in the warm sunlight.
It called to a berry, 'Come join the show!'
But the berry just rolled, saying, 'I'm too slow!'

Then the grape made a plan, fun and astute,
To turn itself into a juicy fruit loot.
With laughter and puns, they began to play,
Creating a vineyard of laughter each day.

Living Fibers

In a world of leafy mischief,
The squirrels dance and prance,
They wear their hats of finest twigs,
And lead a silly, wild romance.

The trees gossip with the breeze,
Whispers rustle through the air,
A leaf caught laughing as it sneezes,
A nature's joke beyond compare.

With roots that wiggle underground,
And vines that tickle every toe,
The playful plants have madly found,
A way to put on quite a show.

So next time you pass by a shrub,
Remember they are sly and spry,
Don't be a timid little grub,
Join in their leafy, laugh-filled cry!

The Heartbeat of Nature

There's a rhythm in the rustling leaves,
A pulse that makes the branches sway,
Beetles marching like tiny thieves,
Stealing sunshine day by day.

With every beat, the flowers giggle,
As bees buzz in a silly tune,
They wiggle, they jiggle, they hardly wiggle,
While playing hopscotch with the moon.

The grass beneath does tickle your feet,
As if it's calling out for fun,
An outdoor party, oh so sweet,
Where laughter dances in the sun.

So join this rhythmic, silly spree,
And let your spirit float and dart,
For nature's heartbeat, wild and free,
Is truly a comical work of art!

Dappled Shadows

In the dappled light, shadows chatter,
As squirrels play peek-a-boo,
Leaves shout out with gleeful splatter,
In the sunny forest zoo.

The sun plays tricks on bumblebees,
Like a jester with a crown,
Buzzing round the dancing trees,
In a jolly, bustling gown.

Frogs croak jokes by the lily pad,
Hopping high with glee and jest,
While dragonflies, with wings so rad,
Buzz in laughter, feeling blessed.

So when you walk in dappled rays,
Just know the fun is all around,
Nature's humor loudly plays,
In sunshine's whispers, joy is found!

Intricate Patterns

Nature weaves with threads so sly,
Patterns twist and turn with glee,
A leafy quilt that dares to fly,
Making art for all to see.

The caterpillar's silly shimmy,
Leaves giggle with every sway,
In this garden filled with whimsy,
Where laughter grows like flowers play.

Twisting vines of tangled bliss,
Climbing high on silly walls,
With every curve, a joyful kiss,
As sunlight dances, laughter calls.

So marvel at this playful design,
Intricate patterns, nature's jest,
Where every leaf and petal shine,
In a grand show of fun, not rest!

Symphony of Shades

In a world of broccoli and peas,
The vegetables dance like a summer breeze.
Carrots sing high while cabbage brings low,
Radishes giggle, putting on a show.

A cucumber slips in with a suave little grin,
Lettuce joins in, and the party begins.
Kale busts a move, all dizzy and bright,
While potatoes roll by, to everyone's delight.

Broccoli flirts, wearing a crown made of cheese,
As bell peppers shimmy with utmost ease.
Zucchini twirls with rhythm and flair,
While onions cry laughter; it fills up the air.

And when the sun sets on this veggie parade,
They gather around for a fresh lemonade.
A toast to the greens, with a wink and a laugh,
In this jolly garden, they dance on the grass.

Echoes of Renewal

A snail on a leaf thinks he's quite a thinker,
While ants all around say, "Dude, you're a stinker!"
They're busy exchanging their secrets of toil,
As worms giggle softly, all covered in soil.

The daisies play tricks with the young little bees,
Announcing they're hiding with flares of bright tease.
"Come find us!" they chant, "We'll buzz 'til you're sore,
But good luck on our trail, it's a pollen galore!"

A frog on a lily just crossed his big legs,
Watching the antics of flowing green pegs.
The fish all conspire below with a splash,
While turtles just chuckle, slow and unabashed.

From roots pop the jokes as the vines start to sway,
With laughter contagious, they brighten the day.
The echoes of cheer rise up to the sky,
Nature's own comedy, a giggly reply.

Embrace of the Thicket

In a thicket so thick, where the shadows play tricks,
Squirrels hold meetings, all sharing their picks.
"Let's hide away nuts!" a wise one suggests,
While nearby a rabbit just want to be blessed.

The bushes all rustle, a committee of green,
While the flowers complain they're out of the scene.
"Let's make up a rhyme!" says one cheeky bloom,
"I'm tired of waiting, come join in the room!"

The trees form a chorus, leaves dancing around,
Shaking their branches, their laughter profound.
"Why do we stand here, just whispering 'hi'?"
As the thicket giggles, a laugh multiplies.

And when the sun sets, the night comes alive,
With crickets composing their own lively jive.
In the embrace of the thicket with critters so spry,
The forest's a party, no need to be shy.

Underneath the Canopy

Underneath the canopy, shadows play games,
Where critters all gather, no need for last names.
A raccoon organizes a feast of delights,
Pinecone pizzas and leaf-dappled bites.

The squirrels all laugh, tossing acorns in cheer,
While a wise old owl hoots, "I'll judge the dessert!"
Mice, with their antics, build castles in twigs,
And dance 'round the herbs like they're wearing their digs.

A hedgehog rolls in, all spiky and round,
He's dancing the tango with moves that astound.
Frogs leap in puddles, making the splash,
While everyone giggles, longing to dash.

As the stars glimmer softly like dots on a wall,
A toast is proposed to the fun-loving thrall.
"Here's to the canopy, wild and carefree,
In this mix of mischief, where all can agree!"

Serpentine Paths of Growth

Worms in suits twist and twirl,
As seedlings strut with vibrant whirl.
A cabbage rolls, with zest and glee,
While radishes gossip under the tree.

Jolly daisies sway with flair,
Tickled by the breeze in their hair.
A carrot dreams of a tap dance show,
And rhubarb joins with a lively growl!

Sunlight chuckles, shadows play,
A garden party every day.
With trowels raised like 'just for fun',
Each plant a joker, everyone!

So let us skip along the rows,
Where nature paints in funny strokes.
A cucumber jokes, "I'm quite a pickle!"
In this hilarity, life's a tickle!

The Garden's Silent Pulse

In quiet corners, mischief brews,
A pumpkin dons a pair of shoes.
Lettuce giggles, trying to dress,
And peas perform a shuffle, no less!

The soil hums a whimsical tune,
As ants in tuxedos dance by the moon.
Cabbages gossip in leafy tones,
While onions sigh in their rooted zones.

A sly fox steals a tomato snatch,
But oh, it's caught in a lemon patch!
With laughter echoed 'round the plots,
Each sprout a jester in its spots!

So let them dance, shout, and sing,
A garden's heart is a cheeky thing.
In sync with laughter, they expand,
A world of whimsy, completely unplanned!

Shades of Nature's Resilience

In hues of laughter, colors blend,
A violet flower plays pretend.
With dandelion hair blowing wild,
It mimics a carefree, giggling child.

Oh, how the beetroot blushes bright,
When asked if it's a squat little sprite!
While sunflowers boast of their lofty ways,
Turning heads and soaking rays.

Even the shyest herbage peeks,
Whispering secrets and little tweaks.
In the garden's embrace, what joy is found,
Where each sprout and seedling spins round!

So let's believe in silly dreams,
Through every wink and giggle gleams.
In every patch, a story we find,
Of nature's humor, beautifully designed!

Understories of Life's Embrace

Beneath the leaves, a squabble brews,
Where critters argue over their dues.
A hedgehog claims, "I'm the best at rolling!"
While mushrooms giggle, cheerily folding!

A ladybug, all decked in spots,
Holds court with ants in funny plots.
"Who can carry the biggest crumb?"
While grasshoppers leap with a cheeky hum!

The roots are whispering wise old jokes,
That even the branches can't help but coax.
In this lively underbrush, fun unfurls,
With nature's laughter, the world twirls!

So if you wander where the shadows play,
Be sure to listen to what they say.
In this merry throng of earthy bliss,
Every moment's a giggle, don't miss!

Rows of Revival

In the garden, beans dance high,
Tomatoes giggle as they pass by.
Lettuce plays hide and seek,
While carrots blush, feeling chic.

Sunflowers wear their crowns with glee,
Waving to bees, 'Come sip some tea!'
A radish roars, 'I'll grow with flair!'
The veggies join in laughter, rare.

Everything's sprouting, what a sight,
Even the weeds want in on the fight.
Each plant struts in a lively prance,
In rows so neat, they all advance!

They gossip about the morning dew,
And plot mischief—oh, who knew?
When gardens take a funny spin,
Life's more fun when greens begin!

Enchanted Growth

A pumpkin winks from the vine,
Saying, 'I'm the star, see me shine!'
Zucchini joins in with a pun,
'Fry me up; I'm lots of fun!'

Radishes roll like they're bowling,
Peas in pods laughing, controlling.
Carrots wear shades to soak up sun,
And declare, 'This day is just begun!'

Herbs are whispering secrets sweet,
Basil and thyme can barely compete.
Chives are snickering, sprouting tall,
In this enchanted world, they have a ball!

Watch as they share wild stories bold,
Of how they sprouted from seeds of old.
In this patch of humor, they thrive,
Creating laughter, keeping joy alive!

Nature's Network

Roots are chatting, underground,
'What's the latest gossip found?'
Fungi giggle, playing tricks,
While everyone hums with happy flicks.

Grass blades gossip, 'Watch us sway!'
They're stoked for rain, 'Hip-hip-hooray!'
Squirrels by the oaks take flight,
Daring each other to take a bite.

The flowers scheme in colors bright,
'Let's make a dance party tonight!'
A daisy shimmies, skips along,
While thistles hum their prickly song.

Nature's crew is all so spry,
In this quirky dance, they fly high.
A network of smiles in every green,
Making the world a little more keen!

Fertile Patterns

Wiggly worms in fashion show,
Strutting their stuff in soil, you know!
With patterns elegant, almost a tease,
They wiggle and squirm, oh what a breeze!

Cabbage layers its frilly fan,
While beets roll out a rooty plan.
Pumpkins juggle under the sky,
With squash on the side, oh me, oh my!

Patterns of growth, a playful sight,
Floral confetti, pure delight.
Chard and celery swap their styles,
Creating laughter, wide-eyed smiles.

Nature's quilt, stitched with glee,
Each plant a comedian, don't you see?
In this fertile land, humor reigns,
Where every leaf shares playful gains!

Harmony in Hues

In a garden where colors collide,
The daisies wear pink, the grass tries to hide.
Butterflies dancing, what a funny sight,
They hiccup with joy, then take off in flight.

The sun wears a smile, so bright on the land,
While worms in a conga line wiggle and stand.
The trees crack jokes, as they sway in the breeze,
Tickling the leaves, with such effortless ease.

Bumblebees giggle, buzzing with flair,
They steal all the nectar, not a single care.
A wily old snail races, slow on his game,
Claiming he's fast, yet none know his name.

With hues intertwined, chaos is king,
A riot of colors makes every heart sing.
In this vibrant place, laughter runs free,
A carnival buzzing, oh what a spree!

The Tides of Terrain

The mountains are rolling, what a sight to see,
They're giggling and bouncing like kids on a spree.
Rivers are racing, splashing with glee,
Waterfalls chortle, 'Come play, come be!'

The clouds wear their fluffy hats, oh so grand,
Making puns about the land, hand in hand.
Rain falls like jokes, not a care in the storm,
The puddles reflect, each mischief they form.

The rocks tell tales, clattering in cheer,
As squirrels pull pranks, shedding seeds far and near.
The grass tickles toes, with a playful tease,
Nature's own giggles wafting through the trees.

With laughter echoing off every hill,
The creatures unite, a riotous thrill.
In the tides of the terrain, joy is the key,
A carnival of antics, wild and free!

Linings of Life

In the cloth of the earth, patterns emerge,
With stitches of humor, nature's own surge.
The daisies are buttons, the thorns, they poke,
While life's little quirks tickle, provoke.

The skies are soft quilts, stitched with bright thread,
While the worms make a bed, for naps in the spread.
Every cloud puffs up, laughs with delight,
As they blanket the world, all cozy and bright.

The ants march in lines, like a parade of cheer,
They're hauling their crumbs without any fear.
A toad on a lily, croaks out a song,
Two frogs join in chorus, oh, it won't be long!

Beneath the bright sun, they frolic and play,
In the linings of life, where laughter holds sway.
Each crease and each fold has a tale to share,
In the fabric of nature, joy's everywhere!

Nature's Cartography

With crayons of nature, the earth starts to squiggle,
A map full of giggles, a swirly wriggle.
Where rivers doodle, and mountains make signs,
Each twist and each turn, in playful designs.

They chart out the fun, in colors so bright,
As the sun splashes gold, igniting the light.
The trees wave their arms, like they're cheering a game,
Each branch is a player, but none know their name.

The rolling hills tumble, in laughter they roll,
While birds in the sky take a census of soul.
"Hey, who's that?" they chirp, as they dive and they spin,

Creating a ruckus; oh, let the fun begin!

On this quirky map, all paths intertwine,
A treasure of whimsy, like rich vintage wine.
In nature's own atlas, humor's the key,
A playful adventure, for you and for me!

Roots of Resilience

In the garden, weeds have a ball,
They dance and twirl, they never fall.
With roots so strong, they mock the sun,
Uninvited guests, oh, what fun!

They gossip with the daisies all day,
Plotting mischief in their leafy way.
While tulips sigh, the roses pout,
Those rascally roots know what it's about.

In rain or shine, they take a stand,
Holding secrets in the land.
With courage found in dirt and mess,
These cheeky sprouts, they love to impress.

So if you see a weed parade,
Join in the fun, don't be afraid.
For nature's laugh is wild and free,
In this riot of roots, there's glee!

Chlorophyll Dreams

In a leafy world of shades so bright,
Plants come alive in the moon's soft light.
With dreams of sunshine and morning dew,
They giggle and whisper, 'What shall we do?'

Swaying to tunes of the buzzing bee,
Planning a party beneath the tree.
Buds wear hats made of clover and twine,
Throwing a bash, oh, it's simply divine!

They serve up nectar in fancy cups,
With pollen pastries and petal puffs.
The tree trunk plays DJ, spinning the tunes,
While beetles boogie beneath the moon.

In chlorophyll dreams, laughter abounds,
Celebrating life where joy resounds.
So if you're lost, just look to the leaves,
Join their jive, it's one that deceives!

The Breath of the Soil

Soil has secrets, oh what a tease,
Whispering tales through rustling breeze.
Worms have their meetings and sly little chats,
While daisies chuckle in fancy hats.

Each shovel's dig brings stories to share,
About sprouting joys and rains that care.
The roots gossip low, while the branches hum,
In this underground ball, they're never glum.

With every compost, there's laughter amassed,
Gathering memories of seasons past.
Who knew dirt had a life full of glee?
In the breath of the soil, you'll find jubilee!

So next time you dig, be light on your toes,
The earth's got a punchline, and everyone knows.
Beneath the surface, they play and they twirl,
In this underground world, life's a whirl.

Veiled Verdancy

In the forest, the foliage wears a disguise,
A leafy cloak, oh, what a surprise!
The ferns giggle, the vines swing around,
Whispering jokes in their leafy sound.

With hidden sprouts throwing a show,
They mime their stories, all aglow.
Caterpillars boast of their glittering dreams,
While butterflies chuckle, bursting at the seams.

Under canopies deep, the fun never stops,
As turtles play leapfrog and old woodpeckers bop.
Among shadows and sunlight, laughter runs rife,
In verdant veils, they celebrate life!

So step into the woods, where jest fills the air,
With nature's own laughter, you'll find joy everywhere.
For beneath all the layers, in shades so quaint,
Lies a world that's alive, and it's far from faint!

Veins of the Earth

In the ground, a ticklish flow,
Wiggly roots putting on a show.
They sneeze and giggle underground,
While dancing worms make silly sounds.

Rivers laugh as they twist and wind,
They play peek-a-boo, so hard to find.
Nature's bloodstream, a funny sight,
Frogs leap in, chasing pure delight.

With muddy feet, the trees all cheer,
Their leafy hair's a party here!
They tap their trunks and sway around,
In this green circus, joy abounds!

So when you stroll through leafy lanes,
Hear the laughter in the gains,
The Earth's a jester in disguise,
With goofy roots and smiling skies!

Whispering Leaves

Leaves chattered in a leafy choir,
Sharing secrets, never tire.
A squirrel joins, with nuts galore,
And trips on branches, falls—oh, sore!

They gossip 'bout the sunlit day,
"Did you see the bee ballet?"
A breeze comes by, so cheeky and bold,
Tickling all until they fold.

Oh, how they flutter in the breeze,
Playing hide and seek with ease.
A playful rustle fills the air,
"Come join our fun!" they all declare.

Such laughter in their swaying dance,
With tiny leaves, it's pure romance.
A ticklish, funny, leafy spree,
Just nature's way of being free!

Vital Currents

Bubbles in the brook wear little hats,
Making ripples while chatting with bats.
They tickle toes and splash away,
A water party, come and play!

A frog in croak, a royal decree,
"Hop in quick! Don't miss the spree!"
He juggles pebbles, quite a show,
And everyone laughs at his toe-to-toe!

The current zooms with twists and turns,
While fish practice ballet, in flips and churns.
A splash here, a plop there,
All indulge in the wild affair.

So come, dive in, don't hold your breath,
For in these waters, laughter's the depth.
With every gush and playful swirl,
Nature's pranks make our heads twirl!

The Color of Life

Life's a canvas, painted bright,
With a splash, it feels so right.
The flowers giggle, wearing hues,
Like clowns with polka-dot shoes.

Sunflowers twirl in sunflower hats,
While daisies cheer, "Life's where it's at!"
Petals painting smiles along the way,
Dancing for joy, come what may.

A chameleon tries to join the fun,
But can't decide—red, green, or none?
He blends in with a silly pout,
The best of colors, without a doubt!

In this wacky, vivid display,
Every hue has much to say.
With laughter swirling in every strand,
Nature's palette, oh so grand!

The Symphony of Sprouts

In gardens where the veggies dance,
The carrots sway, they take a chance.
The lettuces play a leafy tune,
While radishes joke about the moon.

Peas chuckle in their little pods,
Onions giggle, hiding their nods.
Tomatoes blush, they're shy and bold,
As garlic spins jokes, quite untold.

Basil twirls in fragrant delight,
Chives and thyme stay up all night.
With every sprout, a story spins,
In this patch where laughter begins.

So grab a fork, let's join this scene,
A salad symphony, fresh and keen.
With every crunch, a joy prevails,
In the garden where humor never fails.

Lively Mines

Deep in the earth, beneath the grind,
Potatoes plot, a cheeky kind.
Carrots dig with tiny shovels,
While beets giggle, making bubbles.

Onions break into a raucous cheer,
Singing songs no one can hear.
Radishes play hide and seek,
In the soil, they laugh and squeak.

Each crop's a joker, bold and spry,
Tickling roots as they wave goodbye.
With muddy boots and sunny rays,
They dance to the rhythm of underground plays.

So when you eat, don't just munch,
Think of the laughter in each crunch.
For in this mine, beneath our feet,
A harvest of hilarity is quite the treat.

Flourished Footprints

In a field of daisies, footsteps bloom,
Each petal giggles, a bright costume.
Clover shapes into silly shoes,
While dandelions play peek-a-boo.

Butterflies jest about their flight,
Wings stroking faces, what a sight!
Bumblebees buzz with jokes so sweet,
Their pollen paths feel like a treat.

Beneath the sun, footprints appear,
Chasing laughter, shedding cheer.
Nature's stage, a comical play,
Where flowers dance in their own way.

So as you roam this funny spree,
Remember all the giggles you see.
In every step, let joy ignite,
For in this bloom, the world feels right.

Urban Jungles

In the city maze, where buildings sprout,
A cactus jokes, there's no doubt.
Traffic lights dance in a funny sync,
While pigeons gossip and sip their drink.

Sidewalks teem with life so bright,
Weeds wear hats, oh what a sight!
A dandelion dreams of a tall skyscraper,
While gum on the ground thinks it's a taper.

Street plants huddle, sharing a grin,
With laughter echoing where they've been.
Sunflowers tall, with stories grand,
Entwine their roots in this wild band.

So when you stroll through this lively scene,
Look closer and find the comic sheen.
In every crack, let chuckles rise,
For in this jungle, humor never lies.

Botanical Echoes of Serenity

In a garden where the ferns like to dance,
A squirrel tried to take a leaf by chance.
It slipped and fell with quite the sound,
And laughed with blooms all around.

The daisies giggled when the sun came out,
While bees in bowties buzzed about.
The broccoli wore a crown, so bold,
Telling tales of veggies old.

The tulips whispered secrets so sweet,
While carrots did the cha-cha on their feet.
In this paradise of plant delight,
The nightingale sang, making it bright.

So when you're feeling down, just know,
There's a botanical world putting on a show.
With laughter sprouting from every seam,
Join the hilarity, live the dream!

Enchanted Flora's Embrace

The daisies wore their brightest hats,
While singing silly songs with the spats.
A butterfly stopped for a quick chat,
But forgot the words—imagine that!

In the shady nook where the vines entwine,
A lizard sat sipping on herbal wine.
He winked at the flowers, all aflutter,
They giggled and blushed, oh, what a clutter!

The thyme spun round with the rosemary,
While spinach tried to dance, oh so merry.
They formed a conga line through the grass,
And even the stones said, "Let's let this pass!"

So join the fray in this leafy shindig,
Where every shrub is a friend, not a pig.
In this charm of petals, lost in the chase,
There's fun in the air; just find your place!

Rebirth in Leafy Whispers

Amidst the leaves where the rabbits prance,
A clover told a joke that made them dance.
A ladybug laughed, tipping her hat,
While a wise old tree just sat and spat.

The moss made a cushion for frogs to relax,
While bees played bingo, plotting their tracks.
A parsnip posed, looking quite regal,
Challenging globes in a veggie sequel.

Amidst chatter of roots and fungi's delight,
The twigs spun tales beneath the moonlight.
They dared the stars to come join their fun,
And tickled the branches, one by one.

So plant a smile and let it grow wide,
In this orchard of laughter, let joy abide.
With every petal and every breeze,
We'll dress our hearts with a leafy tease!

Hidden Channels of Vitality

In the backyard where weeds play peek-a-boo,
A gopher's mistaken for an anxious shoe.
The dandelions snickered, oh, what a sight,
As the tulips debated who'd lead the flight.

The sunflowers bowed, but not for prayer,
They were checking their hair; it was quite the affair.
A handful of mint chimed in with a quirk,
Claiming they're fresh—work, work, work!

The petunias marched in a cartoon parade,
While pumpkins narrated the jokes they'd made.
Around the daisies, the fun never ceased,
As nature's comedians released their beast!

So next time you're down, just peek through the stalks,
Where laughter's hidden in the number of clocks.
Find the whimsy among nature's splendid charms,
And embrace the dialogues of floral farms!

The Dance of Vibrant Chlorophyll

In a world where leaves wiggle and sway,
Photosynthesizing all day,
They throw a party, oh what a sight,
As sunlight waltzes, pure delight.

Laughter bubbles in every frond,
A chlorophyll conga, of which we're fond,
Leaves wear hats made of dew and glee,
Dancing together, wild and free.

The breeze is the DJ, spinning tunes,
With twirls and whirls, like playful loons,
Nature's nightclub under the skies,
Even the insects shake their thighs!

So come to the fest of the leafy brigade,
Where photosynthesis is never delayed,
Let's boogie with roots in this leafy charm,
In the merry grove, where none come to harm.

Nature's Veiled Pathways

In secret trails where shadows meet,
The fungi dance on little feet,
Roots giggle softly 'neath the ground,
A playful world, yet to be found.

The whispers of wanderers pass,
As squirrels in costumes shine like glass,
They play hide-and-seek in every nook,
In a novel that no one's wrote a book!

Branches tickle the clouds with glee,
While busy bees buzz in harmony,
Nature's jesters with routes galore,
Leading us through, forever more.

Come join the fun, leave your care,
In the leafy lanes, breathe the sweet air,
With a wink from the petals, don't you see?
Nature holds laughter, wild and free!

Echoes of Life Beneath the Boughs

Under the arches of shade we roam,
Where creatures conduct an orchestra home,
The roots hum low while the branches sway,
Nature's symphony brightens the day.

Bugs with tiny violins serenade,
While the leaves applaud, a grand parade,
A frog plays piano on a lily pad,
In this lush theater, you can't be sad!

Squirrels play tambourines on the trees,
The chorus of birds sing just for these,
Echoes of joy flit through each branch,
A rollicking jamboree, a leafy dance!

Glimpses of laughter through bark and leaves,
All nature chuckles, it never grieves,
So let the boughs be your joyous guide,
In this echoey realm, let fun reside.

Threads of Renewal in the Underbrush

In the underbrush, a tale unwinds,
With threads of green and playful finds,
Snails ride bicycles made of shells,
Telling anecdotes of their leafy spells.

The ferns gossip under the moon's glow,
While ladybugs waltz to a fast-flowing show,
New sprouts giggle, fresh and spry,
Chasing each other as fireflies fly.

A potpourri of quirkiness flows,
Where soil and sunshine plant their prose,
Roots weaving dreams with a chuckle or two,
A dance of renewal, all bright and new!

So stroll through the brush, take a peek,
In nature's fabric, it's laughter we seek,
With whimsical threads in a light-hearted land,
Join in the frolic, take nature's hand.

www.ingramcontent.com/pod-product-compliance
Lightning Source LLC
Chambersburg PA
CBHW051629160426
43209CB00004B/578